Contents

The toys we play with

What kind of toys do you enjoy playing with?
How would you play with these toys?

Toy designers have to make sure that toys
are safe and strong.

Toys can be designed for a baby,
or a toddler or an older child to play with.

LOOK ■ AROUND ■ YOU

THE
TOYS
WE PLAY WITH

Sally Hewitt and Jane Rowe

Evans

Evans Brothers Limited

About this book

This book has been put together in a way that makes it ideal for teachers and parents to share with young children. Take time over each question and project. Have fun learning about how all sorts of different homes, and the objects in them, have been designed for a special purpose.

The Toys We Play With deals with the kinds of ideas about design and technology that many children will be introduced to in their early years at school. The pictures and text will encourage children to explore design on the page, and all around them. This will help them to understand some of the basic rules about why toys are made from specific materials and are a certain shape, and why they are suited to being played with in a particular way. It will also help them to develop their own design skills.

The 'Eye-opener' boxes reveal interesting and unusual facts, or lead children to examine one aspect of design. There are also activities that put theory into practice in an entertaining and informative way. Children learn most effectively by joining in, talking, asking questions and solving problems, so encourage them to talk about what they are doing and to find ways of solving the problems for themselves.

Try to make thinking about design and technology a part of everyday life. Just pick up any object around the house and talk about why it has been made that way, and how it could be improved. Design is not just a subject for adults. You can have a lot of fun with it at any age – and develop both artistic flair and practical skills.

These toys have been designed for children of different ages.

▶ Ben's toy car is made of soft material.

Would the bus and car below be safe for a baby to play with?

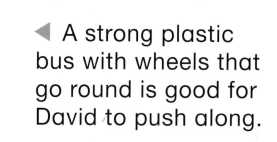

◀ A strong plastic bus with wheels that go round is good for David to push along.

▶ Eddie's car has small parts that can be opened or moved.

This book will tell you about the design of some of the toys you play with.

Baby toys

These toys have been specially designed for babies. Would you find them interesting to play with?

▶ Ruth enjoys listening and looking. She can listen to the mobile play a tune or watch the animals move.

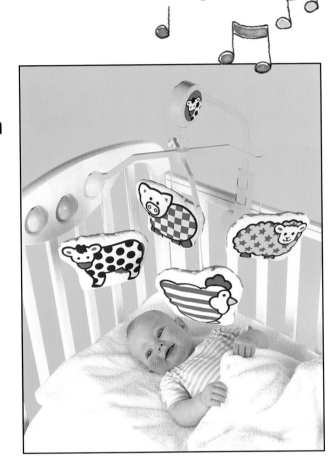

◀ Ben picks up toys and often puts them in his mouth.

Why do you think many baby toys are round and smooth?

Mary is discovering how to post each shape into the right hole.

All these toys are made of plastic. They are washable and unbreakable.

Would metal, paper or wood be good materials for babies' toys?

Eye-opener

These babies' rattles are also 'teethers'.

Babies chew on teethers to help their teeth develop.

One of these rattles is more than 100 years old. Which one?

What differences do you notice between the old one and the new one?

Which part do you think is the teether?

Toys to build with

How many different construction toys can you think of?
What could you use each sort for?

▶ Wooden bricks have at least one flat side, so you can balance them on top of each other.

◀ LEGO® bricks interlock to hold together firmly.

You can use them to make all kinds of complicated models.

How is this
construction toy
different from
LEGO® ?

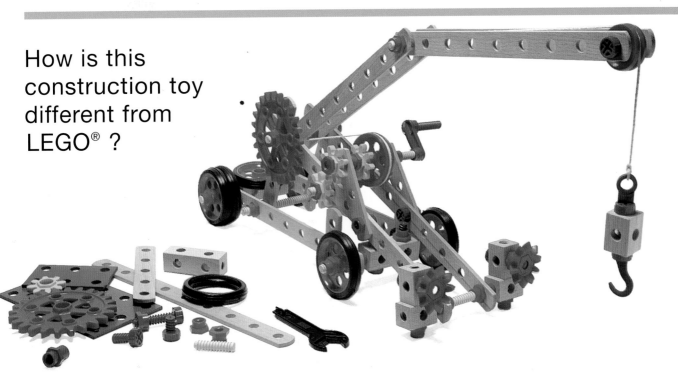

What other kinds of building materials
could you use to make things?

Jane has used card
to make a toy.
What has she made?
Can you see how she has
made it?

Think about what you could
make by slotting pieces of
card together like Jane.

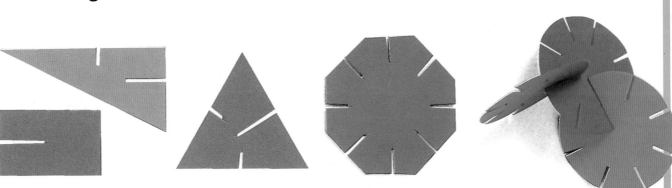

Jigsaw puzzles

How do you work out how to put the pieces of a jigsaw together? You have to look at the shape of each piece and the picture on it.

Put these four puzzles in order, from the easiest to do to the most difficult.

What makes a jigsaw puzzle difficult?

4696-B

Little knobs and simple shapes can make puzzles easy for young children to play with.

This picture is not a photograph of the Empire State building in the United States. It is really a 3D puzzle made of 902 pieces! Here it has been photographed outside to look like a real building.

Your own jigsaw

Copy these pictures onto two pieces of card that are the same size.

Cut them both into nine pieces. Time how long it takes you to do each puzzle.

Which one takes longer?
Can you tell why?

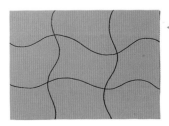

◀You might cut your pieces out like this.

13

Fun with puppets

Puppets are good for making up plays and telling stories. You can make them move and give them voices.

You use your hands to move finger and glove puppets.

Make a glove puppet

1 Fold a piece of felt in half.

2 Put your hand on the felt and draw a body shape round it.

3 Cut out the puppet shape.

4 Sew round the edges, but leave the bottom open.

5 Give your puppet a face, hair and some clothes.

6 Now put it on your hand and start to make it move!

You can make every part of this string puppet move by tilting the bars and pulling the strings.

The audience does not actually see these Javanese puppets. They watch their shadows on a large screen.

Try making shadow puppets by using your hands and a bright light.

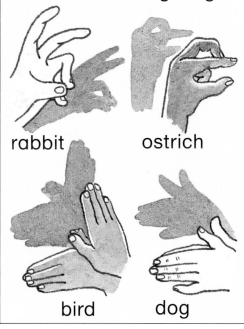

rabbit   ostrich

bird   dog

Which part of the puppet moves when you pull this string?

Board games

Most of the toys in this book can be played with in many ways. Board games are different because they have rules to follow.

The winner of Snakes and Ladders arrives at the 'finish' (100) first. The ladders help you win and the snakes send you backwards.

Players use different coloured counters to move around the board

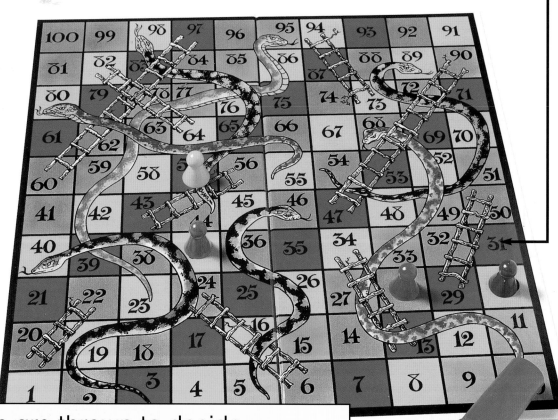

Dice are thrown to decide how many squares you can move. What will happen to the yellow player when he moves along this number of squares?

Design a game

Have fun making up your own game. It could be in a jungle, in space or anywhere you want. If your game is a race, copy this step-by-step road.

Start

1
2
3
4
5
6
7
8
9
10
11
12
13
14
15
16
17
18
19
20
21
22
23
24
25
26
27
2

What kind of counters will you have?

clay shapes

buttons

paper figures

Can you think of any short cuts?

6 13

SWING TO NUMBER 5

What problems might you come across?

SLIP BACK 3 SQUARES

CROCODILE MISS A GO

How will you decide how far you move?

card spinner with colours or numbers

dice

What shape will your board be? Would your game work if the board was shaped like a circle or a triangle?

What other ideas can you think of?

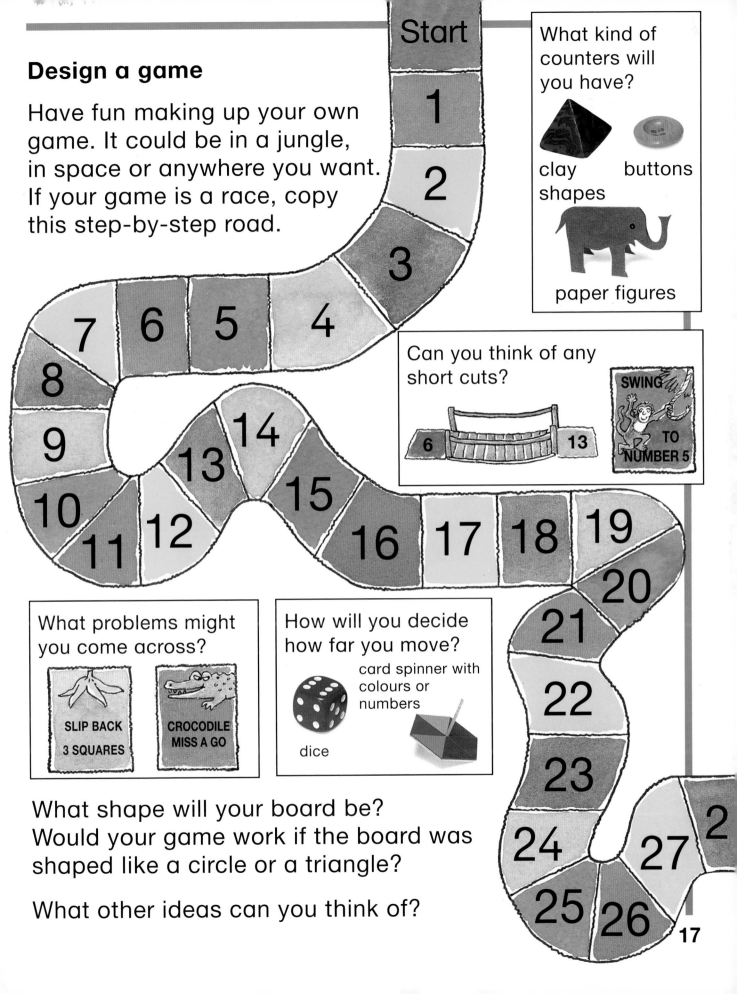

On the move

Some toys are designed to get you moving.

▶ A skipping rope has to be the right length for your height.

The handles must be comfortable to hold.

ball bearings

▲ Ball bearings help the rope to turn quickly and smoothly.

▶ This hopper is made of rubber and filled with air.

Could you bounce around so easily on a square hopper?

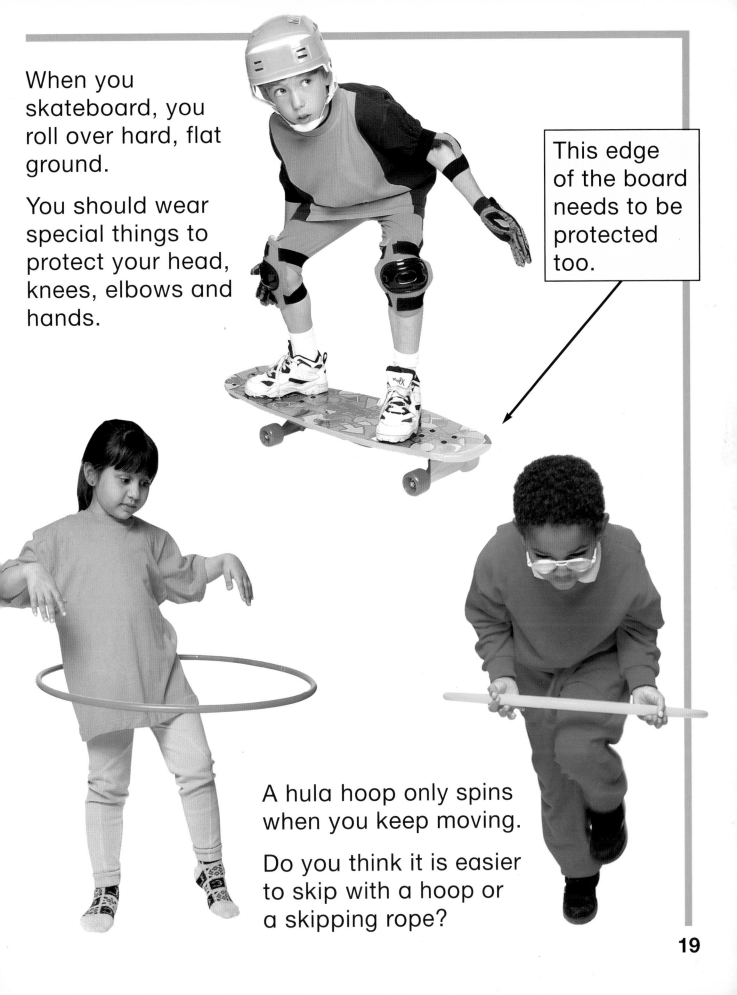

When you skateboard, you roll over hard, flat ground.

You should wear special things to protect your head, knees, elbows and hands.

This edge of the board needs to be protected too.

A hula hoop only spins when you keep moving.

Do you think it is easier to skip with a hoop or a skipping rope?

19

All kinds of balls

People of all ages play ball games.
How many ball games can you think of?

Which of these balls are good for kicking?
Which balls roll but do not bounce?
Which would you find the easiest to catch?
Which ball do you think would bounce the highest?

A hard baseball flies through the air very fast. Why do you need a big padded glove to catch it?

This ball is covered in cloth. It will stick to the velcro pad on one side of the hand bat.

Eye-opener

Try throwing a round ball onto the same spot several times. It will usually bounce in the same direction.

It is difficult to guess how an oval ball will bounce.

Why do you think this is?

Favourite toys

Do you have a favourite teddy,
toy animal or doll?
Does it have a name?
Do you take it to bed
with you at night?

Ed is tightly stuffed to
make him feel firm.
His arms and legs are
movable, so he can
stand up and sit
straight.

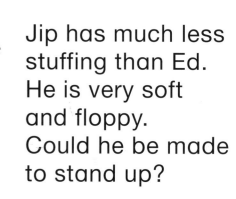

Jip has much less
stuffing than Ed.
He is very soft
and floppy.
Could he be made
to stand up?

Russian dolls are made of wood, painted and varnished.
They fit one inside the other and you can play with them like a puzzle.

Eye-opener

This doll is around 100 years old.
Her china head is easily breakable.
She has real hair and a body made of cloth and stuffing.

How would a child have played with this doll?

Many modern dolls are plastic, with nylon hair.

Which doll would you rather play with?

Playing with water

Which of these toys have been specially designed to play with in water?

What are they made of?

Which of these toys float?
Which pour water?

Which spray water?
Which squirt water?

▶ Why does pouring water into this toy make the wheel go round?

The huge wheels at old-fashioned flour mills are turned by water. As the wheel turns, it moves stones that grind the flour.

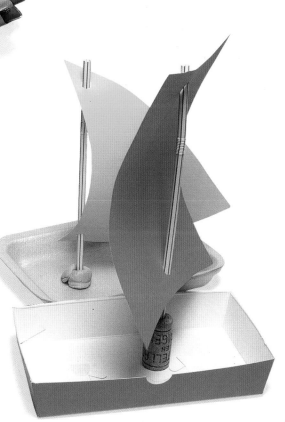

▼ You can look at this book in the bath because it is waterproof and it floats.

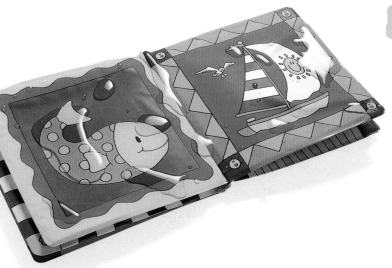

Make one boat from a cardboard box and one from a polystyrene or plastic food tray.

Float them both in a bowl of water. Which one stays afloat the longest?

Kites

Kites are toys to play with on a windy day. They must be made of light material and be the right shape to catch the wind and stay up in the air.

▼ A long tail helps this diamond shaped kite to fly. What else that flies has a tail?

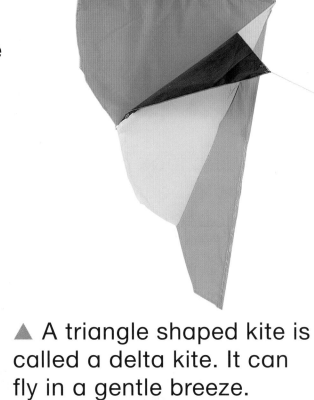

▲ A triangle shaped kite is called a delta kite. It can fly in a gentle breeze.

▶ A box kite with wings flies well in stronger winds. It has more places to catch the wind than a flat kite.

Make a kite that flies

You will need:

A rectangle of plastic, measuring 40 x 30 cm, cut from a carrier bag or refuse bag

2 pieces of thin garden cane, each measuring 46 cm

Wide double-sided tape

A big needle

Strong thread, including 3 pieces measuring 30 cm each

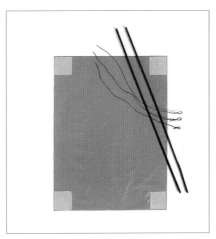

1 Tie a loop in one end of each thread. Stick a piece of tape onto each corner of your plastic sheet.

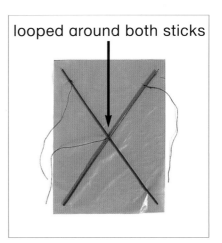

looped around both sticks

2 Put the loops over the sticks. Peel the backing off the tape. Press the ends of the crossed sticks down.

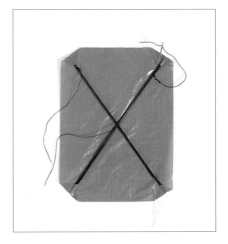

3 Turn the corners over. Ask an adult to help you get the threads to the other side with a needle.

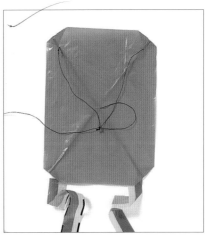

4 Knot the threads together. Tie a very long thread to the knot. Stick on long plastic strips as tails.

5 See how your kite flies! Make your tails as long as possible. What happens when they are too short?

Amazing designs

Look how imaginative the designers have been with their ideas, shapes and materials for these toys!

This pig looks like a normal soft, cuddly toy.

In fact, she is designed to hold your hot water bottle.

◀ Is this is an ordinary rocking chair?
Just like the pig, it isn't what it seems.

The chair is only a few centimetres tall!
It is ideal for fitting inside a really beautiful doll's house.

▲ Dino the dinosaur has a baby that pops out of the egg as you move her along in your bath-water.

▲ Can you see what else happens when Dino and her baby get wet? If you can't see, the answer is on page 30.

A boomerang comes right back to you when you throw it.

This boomerang is made of special soft material, so that you can throw it indoors.

Next time you are playing with your toys, think about how they have been designed. Think up toy ideas of your own, and make them if you can!

Index

Answer to page 29:
Dino and her baby turn a much paler colour when they have been soaking in warm water.